Erhard Zauner

New Ten Commandments
– Ten Mindfulnesses –
for the Time of and after Covid-19

Erhard Zauner

New Ten Commandments – Ten Mindfulnesses – for the Time of and after Covid-19

A draft for new, generally applicable commandments that can serve as an ethical guideline for all people regardless of their religion or belief

First published in German; title of the original:

Neue Zehn Gebote
– Zehn Achtsamkeiten –
für die Zeit von und nach Corona

Bibliografische Information der Deutschen Nationalbibliothek:
Die Deutsche Nationalbibliothek verzeichnet diese Publikation
in der Deutschen Nationalbibliografie; detaillierte bibliografische
Daten sind im Internet über dnb.dnb.de abrufbar.

Bibliographic information from the German National Library:
The German National Library records this publication
in the German National Bibliography; detailed bibliographic
Data can be called up on the Internet at dnb.dnb.de.

Herstellung und Verlag (Manufacture and publishing): BoD – Books on Demand,
Norderstedt

ISBN 978-3-75-433943-5

I thank all people
who have contributed
that this book could appear.

I dedicate this book to all people
who do not want to be dictated
what to believe.

Contents

Introduction

For fifty years I have been dealing with questions of the history of religion and the philosophy of religion, especially in the Judeo-Christian area. Since I grew up without religious beliefs and dogmatic influences from birth, it is much easier for me to approach completely neutral and open questions that lie in the border area of religion, philosophy and history. In the course of my studies of the Bible, of course, I also analyzed the Ten Commandments and came across a number of inconsistencies. On closer inspection it became clear that the classic Ten Commandments of the Bible do not meet the requirements that are made of universal ethics. They are absolutely sexist, xenophobic, unbalanced, and not shaped by the all-encompassing "divine love" that is always emphasized by the church. On the other hand, the biblical commandment to love one's neighbor has found no place among the ten (most important) commandments, neither in the first nor in the second version. In addition, charity is not an invention of Jesus or Christianity, because this is already anchored in the Old Testament (OT).

(Lev 19:18) ... but thou shalt love thy neighbour as thyself

This commandment to love one's neighbor is, however, quoted several times in the New Testament (NT) in different contexts. Particularly noticeable, however, is the passage where Jesus extends charity to love one's enemies. He depicts charity as something actually very banal, since, in his opinion, it is not worthwhile to love those who love you too. In my opinion, an impermissible restriction or shortening is made. In the original statement *"Thou shalt love thy neighbour as thyself"*, no distinction is made between whether the neighbor also loves you or not, whether he is a friend or an enemy. In my opinion, the commandment to love one's neighbor in the OT already includes love of one's enemies, while Jesus unnecessarily only reduces it to "dear neighbors".

(Mat 5:43) Ye have heard that it hath been said; Thou shalt love thy neighbour, and hate thine enemy. (44) But I say unto you, Love your enemies, bless them that curse you, do good to them that hate you, and pray for them which despitefully use you, and persecute you; (45) That ye may be the children of your Father which is in heaven: for he maketh his sun to rise on the evil and on the good, and sendeth rain on the just and on the unjust. (46) For if ye love them which love you, what reward have ye? Do not even the publicans the same?

The very first commandment mentioned in the Bible is: *"Be fruitful, and multiply, and replenish the earth, and subdue it: and have dominion (...) over every living thing that moveth upon the earth."* (Gen 1:28) is also not part of the Ten Commandments. However, the second part, subjugating and ruling, was sometimes very excessively practiced, which on the one hand led to the exploitation of the earth and on the other hand to inhumane industrial animal production, since animals are simply seen as a "thing" over which one rules.

Based on this knowledge that the biblical Ten Commandments were inadequate, the idea arose to design a new, comprehensive and balanced version of the Ten Commandments for all people of all faiths but also for non-denominational and so-called "unbelievers".

Therefore, it seemed to me sensible and important to find a contemporary and universally valid version of the Ten Commandments that can be accepted by people of different religions

10

as well as by agnostics. So that no wrong impression arises, I do not want to measure myself against God, if there is one at all, especially not with the vengeful Yahweh, the God of the Bible, who considers himself responsible only for the descendants of Jacob. These are human commandments for "free disposal"; there are no penalties for non-compliance, neither threatened nor executed. Nobody has to leave his faith, nor does one have to join a "new religious community", because with my Ten Commandments – Ten Mindfulnesses – there is no creed, no religion, no church contribution and no dogmas.

I originally planned to use the title of this book as "The New Ten Commandments – Ten Mindfulnesses – for the 21st Century." The occurrence of the covid pandemic – about the medical necessity or economic and political motivation of which I do not want to comment further – represents a dramatic impact in many people's lives. This leads to many questioning a lot or looking for a new orientation. Therefore, I have now added the addition "for the time of and after Covid-19" to the book.

I have not formulated my commandments either as an exclusive request "You should" or as a prohibition "You should not", because the coexistence of people in society is much more differentiated than being divided into "good and bad" deeds separate, nor regulate with "commandments and prohibitions". My commandments are calls for everyone to be aware of the effects of what one does. That's why I prefer to call them "mindfulnesses". Nevertheless, I have referred to them in the book title as "Ten Commandments" so that this book can be classified and assigned to the corresponding topic at first glance.

I have deliberately formulated the new commandments very briefly and concisely so that they are easy to remember and can

11

be applied as far as possible. I add exemplary explanations to the individual commandments in order to get to know my thoughts that led to the respective formulation and to better understand what is meant by them. But these are by no means exhaustive, because I do not want to elaborate, define or even prescribe them in the sense of a philosophical or theological system down to the finest detail. I will also give analogies and references to the classic biblical commandments in order to show that all those parts that are of timeless validity are also included in mine, whereby these go far beyond that. I will also point out what I consider to be unnecessary and nonsensical restrictions of the biblical commandments. The purely theological precepts of worship and ritualistic acts are completely absent from me, because in my opinion they have no general validity but are only specific to religion or denomination and only serve to subordinate the believers to the priests. So they can subjugate and dominate the people and can live at their expense (sometimes very feudal).

If you write down the new Ten Commandments in a clockwise circle, the first five mindfulnesses concern you as an individual person and your inner world. You go through yourself, your thoughts, emotions and words to the deeds that have manifest effects on the environment. This brings us to the second five mindfulnesses, which concern the various forms and levels of the external world, from material and intellectual property, through the neighbor or the community, life, the environment to the entire universe. It is up to everyone to decide whether one imagines it to be animated or spiritual. Believing people would use the word "God" to refer to it, which is understandable for me, but not absolutely necessary.

If we look at the effects of under-observing or over-observing (I want to ignore the disregard for a moment) of all commandments, we have to find that the observance of each individual commandment affects all other nine commandments more or less, so they all have an inner connection. I even want to go so far that it is not at all possible to actually keep or observe only nine of these new Ten Commandments, and to ignore the tenth, whatever it may be. Disregarding even one commandment also entails at least neglecting the other nine. Maybe it even means that some or all of them are temporarily disregarded as well. Disregarding or neglecting these commandments is not a sin and therefore does not need to be confessed to a pastor. Nor are there threats of illness, death, eternal damnation or agony in hell. If we find in the Old Testament an almost endless list of commandments, non-observance of which is punished with the death of the sinner, then in the Catholic Church there are the seven deadly sins or grave sins that result in the loss of divine grace, exclusion from the kingdom Christ and eternal death in hell.

- Arrogance (pride, vanity, arrogance)
- Avarice (greed)
- Lust (debauchery, indulgence, desire, unchastity)
- Anger (hot temper, anger, vindictiveness)
- Gluttony (excess, intemperance, selfishness)
- Envy (jealousy, resentment)
- Laziness (cowardice, ignorance, weariness, indolence of heart)

If you look at the many scandals that are currently shaking the Church, you may doubt whether the leaders of the church even believe what they preach?

New Ten Commandments
Ten Mindfulnesses

1. Mind Yourself
2. Mind your Thoughts
3. Mind your Emotions
4. Mind your Words
5. Mind your Deeds
6. Mind the Property
7. Mind the Community
8. Mind the Life
9. Mind the Environment
10. Mind the Universe

Mind the Universe

Mind the Environment

Mind the Life

Mind the Community

Mind the Property

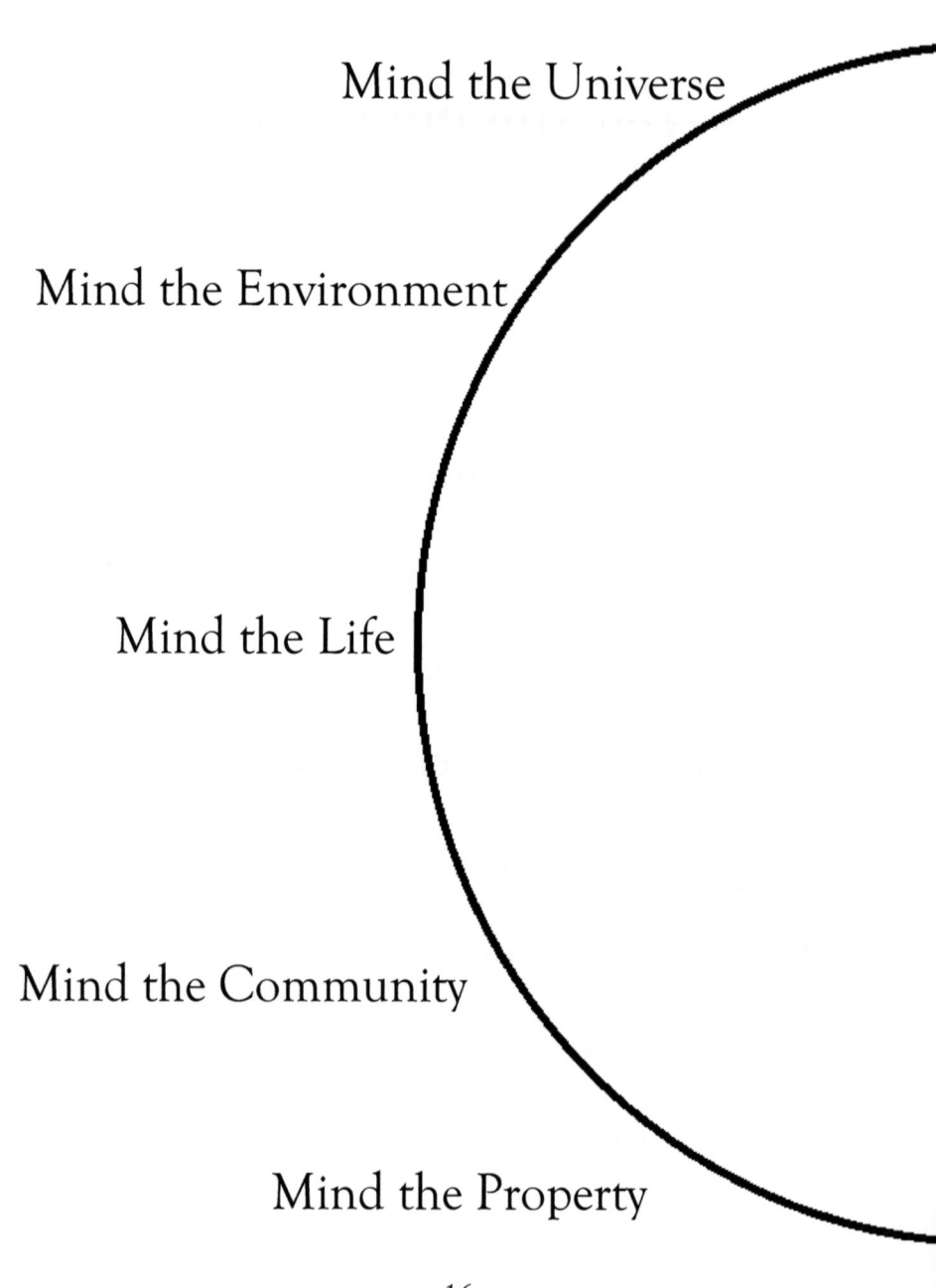

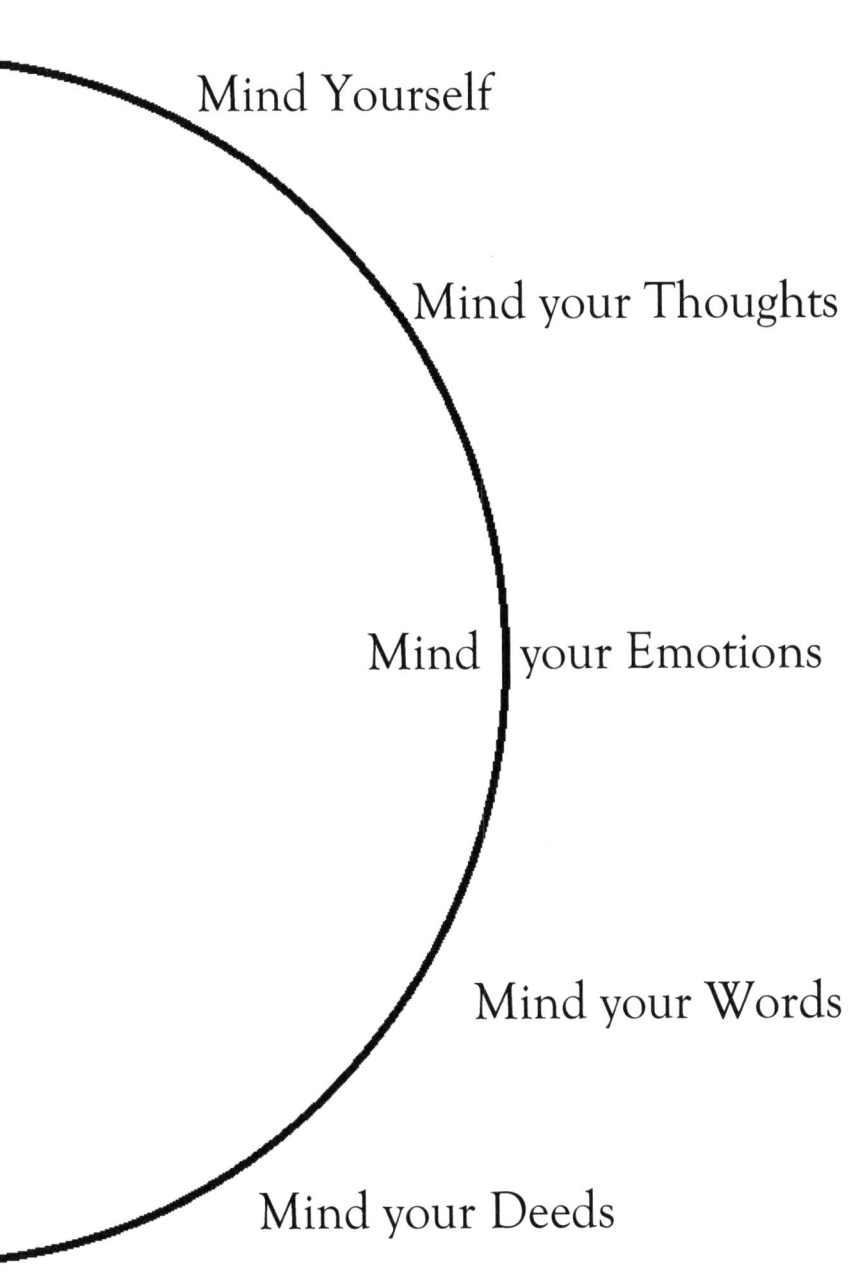

Mind Yourself

Mind your Thoughts

Mind your Emotions

Mind your Words

Mind your Deeds

Preliminary Remarks

I use the expression "mind" in all of my Ten Commandments in the sense of "be attentive to what is happening there", "observe", "pay attention", but also in the sense of "worry and take care of it" or "make yourself aware of the consequences of paying attention or disregarding it". This expression is much less rigorous than "thou shalt" or "thou shalt not", but above all it avoids the resulting consequences. This only makes sense if there are consequences, e.g. penalties, for non-compliance. Here the Catholic Church has created an ingenious instrument for the domination of people by introducing confession. As the ruling power, it has thus induced its ruled subjects to voluntarily report all transgressions. As a reward for the repentant sinners, after a few prayers there was absolution. With hundreds of thousands of pastors worldwide, the Catholic Church probably has the best-staffed information network in the world. Because of the secrecy of confession on the one hand and obedience to the Pope, this informant functioned perfectly for centuries. In case of doubt, the church has understood very well how to use its knowledge of "misdeeds" to exert pressure on its believers if it was of use to the church. On the other hand, the Vatican has never had a problem with dictators, if they were already Catholics and fought against unbelieving communists, as Pope John Paul II's visit to dictator Pinochet in 1987 in Santiago de Chile has eerily demonstrated. This "mind" is a call to the conscience not to do something simply out of habit or out of mere imitation.

First Commandment – First Mindfulness

Mind
Yourself

You will probably be amazed that I put this commandment or this mindfulness first and not last. For me the sequence of mindfulnesses was clear relatively quickly. The question of which is the first and which is the last has preoccupied me for a long time. After careful consideration, I then came to the conclusion that "Mind Yourself" must be placed at the beginning. How could you mind all the other things if you did not mind yourself. But this is no license for ego-centrics or narcissists, because they have an excessive focus on themselves and neglect the respect for everything else, especially for their fellow human beings.

This "Mind Yourself" sounds similar to the biblical "love your neighbor as yourself". Loving and respecting are similar but also different. The opposite pole of love is hate. There are probably relatively few people you really love and even fewer people you really hate. But there are many many people that you neither love nor hate. The request to love your neighbor as yourself easily leads to a utopian attitude: "We are all brothers, we are all dear, and there are no crimes in our world!" But if self-love is rather modest or even not at all pronounced, then the love that is bestowed on one's neighbor is only very modest too.

The statement "Mind Yourself" basically states that you are the one who has to take care of yourself. Why should those around you respect you if you don't respect yourself? Pay attention to your health, your diet, your family life and your circle of friends, your education and professional career, your worldview or religion, etc. etc. However, this also means that in unpleasant situations you do not primarily

22

seek the "blame" on someone else. Whereby, in my experience, it is hardly ever a question of guilt, but rather the question of the cause. You surely know the saying: "Everyone is the smith of their own happiness!" You are not only responsible for your happiness, but also for your unhappiness, for your whole life in general.

If you mind yourself, you will mainly base your decisions on your values and not on the wishes of others. Then you no longer allow yourself to be so strongly influenced by peer pressure or advertising, but live more and more a self-determined life. This will make you more balanced and satisfied, and you will not be thrown off course so easily in the event of unpleasant events. If you can change the situation, change it powerfully! If there is no way you can change it at all, or at the moment, bear it with patience! Aggression, fury and anger only cost a lot of strength, in many cases only worsen your situation without improving anything. Sometimes, you even become blind to opportunities for improvement that arise over time. Annoying means making a situation that is already bad even worse. The cause of your anger usually does not notice it. But with that we come to the next mindfulness.

Mind

your

Thoughts

It is well known that thoughts are free. That is true, but thoughts basically have two tendencies. On the one hand they strive to realize themselves and on the other hand they attract other people who harbor similar thoughts. Just think about how many thoughts, ideas, wishes and conceptions you get inoculated from outside in the course of just one single day? These are not only the thousands of advertising messages from industry and politics, but also the many conscious or unconscious expressions and comments from your fellow human beings. If this "thinking ahead" of the others did not lead to (unconscious) "re-thinking" or "re-flecting" in you, advertising would be ineffective. When a thought, an idea, or an imagination is repeated enough times, we automatically take it as true. Such ideas naturally work much faster and more effectively in children where critical awareness is not yet developed or is not sufficiently developed. Now you will probably understand why practically all religious communities begin the mental imprinting – or should I say indoctrination? – in the earliest days of children, because then these people hang on an invisible leash. How many people do you think would become members of the Catholic Church today, for example, if they could only join the faith as adults, as was customary 2000 years ago?

One of the core tenets of journalism is: "Only bad news is good news". What is meant by this is that the reports of "Sex and Crime" bring considerably more circulation, listeners or viewers and thus advertising income than good news. I don't want you to only look at the world through

26

rose-colored glasses that would be just as unrealistic and also not beneficial for your well-being. But think about how much of the "bad news" you really have to include, how many are really absolutely necessary and indispensable for your decisions and lifestyle. Try to decide for yourself which and how many thoughts, ideas or advertising messages can be conveyed to you from outside or imposed on you. But what you can determine yourself in any case, are all those thoughts that you think out of yourself. This of course also includes deciding which books to read, which films to watch and which people to talk to about which topic. But also note that thoughts, regardless of whether they were thought by yourself or brought to you from outside, not only "float freely in space", but also cause reactions on another level.

Thought impulses – ideas – are the starting point for all deeds, but it is well known that thoughts alone are not enough to move anything even a millimeter. Even the much-vaunted will does nothing in most cases, because it is mostly just an idea, wishful thinking. This is comparable to the prospect of a beautiful vacation home. You can "dream yourself into" this place, but to really get there you have to muster a good amount of energy and a really firm determination to do something. In our case, our feelings are the power and the engine for the implementation of thoughts and the achievement of – ideally self-set – goals. This brings us to the next mindfulness.

Mind your Emotions

If we look again at the bad news from the previous chapter, e.g. reports of crimes, these also create feelings in us. We fear and get mad, get angry, or feel faint. If the thoughts, ideas or conceptions give the direction, so to speak, then the feelings are the power that drives us in this direction, or the brake that paralyzes us. By feelings I don't just mean the "big feelings" that we become aware of, such as contentment, fear, anger, love, loneliness, hope or hopelessness. Above all, I mean those little feelings or fluctuations in feelings that always occur when we experience, do or think something. We mostly perceive feelings as a reaction to some situation, i.e. to a consequence of something that we cannot influence. For most of us, feelings belong to the subconscious.

If I now ask you to "Mind your Feelings", then you will perhaps answer: "How should I do that when they arise in the unconscious area?" It is true, you cannot let a feeling arise at will. But there is a simple connection. The more you occupy yourself with something that scares you, the stronger the fear becomes and, under certain circumstances, it can escalate into panic, which you can then no longer escape. In principle, this also applies to all other feelings. But that means nothing else than that you indirectly have a possibility to control your feelings, quite simply by doing this, depending on what you are dealing with. In the course of the covid-19 pandemic in particular, very strong fears were fueled by the government, which after a short time proved to be largely unfounded. Nevertheless, many people are still affected by these intangible fears in their deeds.

But there is also another aspect that is interesting. I would like to illustrate this to you with a small thought experiment. Imagine there is a beautiful bowl full of sun-ripened Sicilian lemons on the table. You take one of them, bring it to your nose and inhale the wonderful scent of these sun-ripened lemons. You take a sharp knife and halve the lemon; you divide one half again and then take that quarter in your hand. You slowly bring this lemon wedge to your mouth; you smell the wonderful scent of these sun-ripened Sicilian lemons even more intensely than before. You open your mouth and take a hearty bite into the lemon and its sweet and sour juice splashes into your mouth. In anticipation of the coming lemon juice, your body and your salivary glands have already reacted. There is no lemon! You only imagined it. The amazing thing about this is the fact that, even for a manifest physical reaction, it doesn't really matter whether the lemon is really there, or whether you just imagined it. The difference is usually only in the intensity. In other words: feelings are too generated through the imagination, which you can consciously control with your thoughts. The more you deal with it, the stronger your feelings become. It is now up to you whether you "feed" fear, loneliness and hopelessness and thus reinforce them, or whether you generate love, contentment, confidence and hope. Negative feelings weaken your performance and your immune system, make you depressed and sick. Positive feelings strengthen your energy and your health. Therefore pay attention to your feelings, because they modulate your words and are the engine for your deeds and thus for your whole life.

Fourth Commandment – Fourth Mindfulness

Mind
your
Words

It doesn't just matter what you say, but how you say it. "The sound makes the music" is the popular saying. How often has a single word uttered quickly (thoughtlessly) become the cause of a quarrel or argument! I believe that there are no thoughtless words, but that these are words that were not controlled or formulated by conscious thoughts. The automatic area of the brain, the subconscious, triggered a verbal reaction in combination with the emotional world. In many cases, these are characterized by fear or aggression and thus often trigger a corresponding reaction. The conversation, which in itself started peacefully, turns into an argument and then into a fight. It is no longer a question of who is right and who has the better arguments, but only about defeating the other! Once a word like this has escaped your mouth, it is usually very difficult and time-consuming to find your way back to a normal basis of conversation. While thoughts and feelings mostly only take place inside you and can only be perceived or at least suspected by others in your posture or facial expression, the words are direct contact with the environment. The expression "words" here represents the entirety of interpersonal communication, including tone of voice, speed of speech, facial expressions, gestures and body language. Many misunderstandings arise solely from the fact that the other person is mentally different from you. When you start to speak, all related thoughts and feelings, memories and experiences are present for you at the same time that are associated with what you are saying. The other person only hears the few sentences that you are effectively speaking. It therefore makes sense if you use a few words or sentences to mentally lead your counterpart into the area that you want to talk to him about now. Conversely, it makes sense to ask if something seems unclear to you.

On the one hand, words can inspire, but on the other hand they can also quickly hurt someone, i.e. they can sometimes trigger very violent feelings in others. This also includes the area that regulates the biblical command "Thou shalt not bear false witness against thy neighbour", shortened in Christian terms to "you shall not lie". Unfortunately, the absolute condemnation of untruth is theoretically sensible and understandable, but in practice it is not entirely unproblematic. This should not mean that I favor lying, but in many cases smaller or larger deviations from the "naked truth" are not only meaningful for living together, but sometimes even socially directly required. If all people ALWAYS told the truth and nothing but the pure truth, then we would have a permanent war of all against all and probably humanity would have perished as a result.

However, especially in the wake of the covid-19 crisis, I increasingly found that, contrary to the weighing of different approaches and viewpoints customary in scientific discourse, in many cases "truths" postulated by politicians even with laws that target questionable wise came about, are brutally executed. This is usually an unmistakable sign of dictatorships as we know them from the former Soviet Union or China, but should be impossible in democracies. So pay attention to your words.

Mind

your

Deeds

Every deed that you take ultimately has its starting point in a thought, whereby it is completely irrelevant whether you have consciously thought it willingly, as an involuntary reaction to information that you have received, or as a result of targeted manipulation through advertising, economy, press, politics or religion. Not to be forgotten is the influence of family, friends, work colleagues or neighbors in this regard. Many thoughts only light up briefly like a shooting star and then burn up, never to be seen again. Many are doomed to failure just by the mental opening credits "... actually I should..." Other, mostly whispered, impairments (actually: knockout factors) are: "If it were that easy, everyone would do it!", "You can never do it!", "You probably think that you are smarter than everyone else!", "I've already tried that and failed – spare yourself this experience!"

Although we generally think that we do most of our deeds consciously and willingly, the reality is very different. And that's still a good thing. Namely, all more complex recurring activities such as driving a car are almost exclusively controlled by our subconscious. Our consciousness and the voluntary decision are almost only used to decide "when" and "where" we want to go. Or in atypical critical situations for which there are no stored habits or routines. In doing so, we often make conscious decisions that are really not optimal. Therefore, it makes sense, among other things, to do driver safety training, where one is made aware of how to act correctly in certain dangerous situations and this is also practiced several times so that it can be rewound as a standard program by the subconscious.

So we do a lot in exactly this way, because we've always done it that way, because everyone does it that way, or because we don't know any other way. Often, however, we impair or injure other people with our deeds without us being immediately aware of it. This often leads to offense to the other person and thus to a disruption of the relationship. Sometimes this is also consciously accepted in the hope that the other will not find out about it. I just want to mention the keyword affair here.

Except in situations where we are under orders, we are completely free to choose what we do, how we do it, and whether we do it at all. Unfortunately, we use this freedom far too seldom – and I of course also include myself here.

With your deeds you show the relationships with your fellow men, you change and shape your environment. But you are no longer as free as you are with your thoughts, because there are social conventions and traditions on the one hand and rules and laws on the other. These are sometimes incomprehensible and not understandable either. However, there is generally no other option than to stick to it. The only, albeit very laborious and hardly promising, way is to try to change such laws. These are the five mindfulnesses for which we are solely responsible and which we can control entirely from within ourselves. The next mindfulnesses concern our being in the world and our interaction with it.

Mind the Property

This commandment is much more comprehensive than the two biblical "Thou shalt not steal" and "Thou shalt not covet thy neighbour's house, thou shalt not covet thy neighbour's wife, nor his manservant, nor his maidservant, nor his ox, nor his ass, nor any thing that is thy neighbour's". Because there are many situations where nothing is stolen, but the property of others, but also your own, is not sufficiently respected.

Be it through negligent or willful damage or be it simply through neglect and lack of custody, care and use. How often are things simply thrown away only because they are no longer as beautiful as when they were bought, because they no longer work so perfectly, because the charge of the battery does not last as long, or simply because there is already a new, "better" model?

In no way do I want to prevent you from buying a new cell phone, for example, whenever you feel like it. But before you buy it, think about whether this really is a careful use of the resources, or whether your subjectively greater benefit is really worthwhile. And if so, then maybe consider whether your old cell phone can have a second life before you simply throw it away. It is true that today we live in what is known as a throwaway society. With industrial production becoming more and more efficient, in many cases it is cheaper to buy a new piece than to repair the old one. However, many products are already made with a predetermined breaking point, so that they break after a certain period of time, so that the permanent need for replacement and thus continuous production is ensured. In many cases, however, there is also a careful alternative. Similar products of higher quality, which admittedly are also more expensive, have a much longer lifespan. If you convert the price to the lifetime of the product, these are usually even significantly cheaper than the so-called cheap products. In addition, you have a high-quality product and you don't have to worry about wear and tear or failure, usually at completely unsuitable moments. There is a fitting English saying: "I'm not rich enough to buy cheap things".

By property I do not only mean what is usually referred to as real estate or other property, such as cars, cell phones, laptops, furniture, clothes and the like, but also the intellectual property of individual people, as well as the cultural property, religious and traditional achievements and peculiarities of smaller or larger communities. It is precisely with this intellectual or cultural property that many people find it difficult to respect, especially when they contradict their own views or opinions. However, it is particularly important that this respect is mutual. It cannot and must not be that tolerance is answered with intolerance. In my opinion, there is no absolutely true religion that also reserves the right to defame all people of different faiths as inferior or even to force them to accept this belief – possibly with the use of force or the threat of death.

Mind the Community

It's really interesting that there are no two zebras with the same stripe pattern, that there are no two people with the same fingerprints and the same iris colors in their eyes. Put simply, all people are different, and that's a good thing. But not everyone can and should not have to reinvent the wheel, because otherwise we would all still be at the level of the Paleolithic, if at all. No matter how different we humans are, there are also similarities in origin, language, culture, religion, education, interests, etc. Therefore, there are and have always been communities of different sizes and with different objectives. Probably the smallest community is that of marriage or partnership, then that with the children or with the parents, that of the extended family, the clan, the tribe, the village community, etc.

The "Mind the Community" is much more comprehensive than the often quoted biblical love of neighbor, which is not even contained in the Ten Commandments. But it also goes much further than *"Honour thy father and thy mother"*. As a member of a community, you have to adhere to certain rules so that coexistence is thriving. However, you can also contribute to changing these previous rules or in most cases you can also leave a community if you no longer see yourself as a part of it. Of course, there are times when the rules or habits of two communities to which you belong differ or even contradict each other. Then you have to look for a solution, even if you break away from a community.

Respecting the community not only affects that community to which you belong, but also everyone else. Hence it includes the biblical *"Thou shalt not commit adultery"* as well as

"Thou shalt not covet thy neighbour's house, thou shalt not covet thy neighbour's wife, nor his manservant, nor his maidservant, nor his ox, nor his ass, nor any thing that is thy neighbour's". For me, the slavery of any human dignity is a mockery. Unfortunately, this is not only the thoughts of the OT, where even the Israelites are called by Yahweh as his slaves, Paul also speaks praising slavery!

(Lev 25:42) For they [Israelites] are my servants ['ebed' = slave], which I brought forth out oft he land of Egypt: they shall not be sold as bondmen ['ebed' = slave].

(1 Cor 7:21) Art thou called being a servant? Care not for it: but if thou mayest be made free, use it rather.

Also, the Catholic Church has never had a problem with slavery and serfdom in all the centuries, provided that the rulers were well-behaved Christian. In addition, it contributed a great deal to the fact that knowledge remained hidden behind the monastery walls and that the broad mass of the people were, to a certain extent, spiritually enslaved by ignorance.

Even if slavery officially no longer exists today, I find that, as before, in many countries around the world, and especially in the area of large international corporations, many many people in such economic dependency have to work with sometimes existence-threatening low wages that it is very similar to being a slave. Here the community of employees is far too little respected by the bosses.

Mind
the
Life

The eighth mindfulness "Mind the Life" goes far beyond the seventh "Mind the Community", but also includes this in a certain way. If the seventh commandment is about the mindful coexistence of people and the mindful interaction with them, then the eighth mindfulness affects everything and everyone that lives.

"Thou shalt not kill", or as it is partially translated as *"you shouldn't murder"*, represents only a small aspect of respect for life. If you read the Old Testament carefully, you unfortunately have to recognize that right now this commandment is most often ignored even on behalf of Yahweh. In total, the OT reports no less than 99 wars, acts of war or battles. In most cases with a certain pride, since the Israelites were victorious in most cases.

Respect for life is much more to me than that and cannot be reduced to the question of life or death. Apart from the pure substances earth, rocks, water and air, we are practically always and everywhere surrounded by life. Sometimes more intense than we'd like, especially when it comes to mold, bacteria, viruses or so-called vermin or parasites. If we do not fight (kill) them, then our own life becomes very troublesome or may end prematurely. There has to be a trade-off. But here too, out of zeal, you can quickly shoot far beyond the target and destroy the "pests" in good faith, but at the same time also kill a myriad of beneficial insects or free up space for other no less dangerous microorganisms. In a healthy person, the immune system is able to fight and kill almost all harmful germs on its own. In very many cases symptoms of illness do not even appear, in many cases no medicine is necessary and certainly no so-called "vaccination". The latest list of vaccine damages and deaths is probably longer than the advertised successes.

Respecting life begins with living together in the family and community and ends with respect for all life anywhere in the world. I don't want to praise the vegetarian or vegan diet, nor do I want to snub their advocates. For me it depends much more on the circumstances and attitudes towards killing animals for food. Here, both rearing and slaughtering can be treated with a lot or little attention. Even in the oh-so-peaceful and beautiful nature, there is a completely merciless eating and being eaten in large parts. And in most cases this is a self-regulating mechanism. Unfortunately, this was only broken by humans – out of food envy – by exterminating the wolf, for example. The resulting increase in red deer must now be regulated again by hunters so that it does not destroy the crops. Respect life also means not tormenting, hurting, suppressing or bullying anyone.

Mind the life also means "respect unborn life"! I understand that an unwanted pregnancy after a rape represents an enormous (psychological) problem and that the life of the mother and her relatives is weighed against the life of the unborn child. I hardly understand, however, that with today's contraceptive options, so many abortions are still carried out in intact relationships. From my point of view, there is a lack of respect for life due to thoughtlessness.

51

Mind

the

Environment

The ninth mindfulness "Mind the Environment" goes far beyond the eighth "Mind the Life", but also includes this again in a certain way. If the eighth commandment is about the careful handling of any living being, the ninth commandment simply affects anything and everything that surrounds us, regardless of whether it is animate or inanimate. It includes many topics that are often highlighted by various groups with, in some cases, global actionism. While quite a few claims are justified, at least at first glance, they often turn out to be problematic on closer inspection. It is certainly true that electric cars produce significantly less or no emissions when in use; after all, there is no gasoline or diesel burned. The quantity of climate-damaging gases and environmentally damaging processes that are produced in the manufacture of electric cars and especially batteries, exceeds in some cases by far that of the demonized cars with internal combustion engines. Not to be neglected is the inhumane child labor involved in cobalt extraction. Ultimately, the question also arises: Where should all the electricity come from? It is unsurpassable mockery when politicians suggest that everyone at home should have a diesel-powered generator for it.

The existing power plants are already at their capacity limit and short-term blackouts are the order of the day. More nuclear power plants mean more nuclear waste that has to be kept safe for thousands of years. Generating more electricity from coal or crude oil, in turn, increases fine dust and CO_2 emissions, and there is also a lower level of efficiency than if petrol were burned directly in the car. Ulti-

54

mately, I also ask myself why the oh so "harmful" – actually completely non-toxic – carbon dioxide in the industrial greenhouses is artificially increased to around three times the value so that the plants grow faster? Sugar and starch are carbohydrates, which, as the name suggests, are formed from carbon dioxide and water and are broken down again into these two substances when burned or digested.

Wind power plants produce electricity far too irregularly, which practically cannot be temporarily stored, and the areas suitable for this are far away from the areas where the electricity is needed. Long overhead lines with a very large line loss would have to be built at great expense.

Solar systems on any suitable roof could produce electricity in a decentralized manner and independently of local or national blackouts. If work comes to you at home (home office) instead of driving to work every day in a traffic jam, it could do a lot for the environment as well as your work-life balance and well-being. When dozens or hundreds of people no longer have to jet across the country or the whole world in airplanes at teleconferences, more is done for the environment than at so many Friday-for-Future protest rallies. Buying apples from local cultivation instead of flying fruit from the other side of the world also helps the local economy. These are just a few thoughts on the subject of "respect the environment". Every day, every single one of us has the opportunity to consciously do something for the environment and thus for a better life for ourselves and all people, even with small decisions.

Tenth Commandment – Tenth Mindfulness

Mind
the
Universe

The tenth commandment – the tenth mindfulness – is on the one hand the most comprehensive of all, but on the other hand also the least concrete. By the term universe I do not mean only the physical universe with all its billions of galaxies and stars, but especially all the forces that work in it, regardless of whether we already know them or not, whether we can measure and calculate them or not, whether we believe in it or not. For me it also encompasses the entire area of the ethereal, the soul and the spiritual insofar as it goes beyond the personally individual.

I understand very well when people who emphasize this side, rational, but also materialistic people or especially scientists have a problem with the last statements because they simply do not understand them or have no sensorium for them. On the other hand, there are just as many people, if not significantly more, who understand neither the strong nor the weak interaction, and also not the theory of relativity. You know the effect of electricity, magnetism and gravity, but you cannot explain their physical principles either. What is to be found with them, however, is some form of faith, not necessarily in the sense of a theologically founded religion, but simply a premonition, an assumption or a feeling that there are "more things between heaven and earth than we have with ours Knowing understanding "(Lao Tzu). Or as Hamlet says to Horatio: "There are more things in heaven and earth than your school wisdom (orig.: philosophy) can be dreamed of."

Many scientists have also had suspicions or even experiences like this, often just not daring to make it known publicly because they are of the opinion that their scientific reputation would suffer as a result.

It doesn't really matter whether it is a single, unrestricted ruling god, or only responsible for one's own believers, or a trinity of gods, a fully occupied Olympus with twelve main gods, minor gods, demigods, titans, graces or muses. It is also irrelevant whether it is gnomes, elves, nymphs, fauns, alb, demons, sylphs, forest spirits, trolls, nissors or dwarfs. Angels, archangels, cherubim and seraphim, as well as devils, Satan and Lucifer also belong in this category. Some believe in them, some call them for help or worship them; others see them as the cause of misfortunes and illnesses. For many, these beings, regardless of whether they can be proven or not, are simply part of their lives and also a support.

Whatever or whoever you believe in, try to respect these forces and beings of the universe. Just as you cannot evade the physical laws, e.g. gravity, just as you cannot evade the soul-spiritual beings and laws, if they exist. The word universe is composed of the Latin "unum – one" and "versus – turned". If someone (e.g. you) turns around, then you have captured your entire environment, your universe, even if you have not seen everything until the last infinity. Just try to live in harmony with everything around you, to live in peace and harmony with YOUR universe.

Outlook

Especially in turbulent times, such as the current one, it is important that we do not let ourselves drift aimlessly. Otherwise we become an easy victim of powers that do not want what is best for us but what is best from us, namely our freedom, our sovereignty and our money. It is therefore necessary that we think for ourselves and act confidently. The present new Ten Commandments – Ten Mindfulnesses – are a simple guide to achieve the greatest possible self-determination and at the same time the least possible influence on our fellow human beings and the environment.

Happiness is not a result of hard work or wealth. Happiness is a kind of equilibrium between aspired and achieved goals, work and leisure, time for you and time for others, but also freely available money and open material desires. Unfortunately, the aggressive advertising of the economy has resulted in many people living on the hamster wheel according to the following motto: "They buy things with money that they do not have, things that they do not need in order to impress other people they do not like. By the way, the career path in many professions is also more like a hamster wheel: you have the feeling that you are climbing the career ladder, in fact you just pedal on the spot, and the boss and the owners are happy about your great performance. And if you can no longer make it, then you "may" get off the hamster wheel with your burn-out or heart attack, and the next one gets a chance. Illness can and must never be an adequate price to pay for the achievement of any professional, financial or material goal. Your health is too valuable and unique. Even if modern medicine can work wonders in many cases, maintaining natural health is still far more useful than restoring it.

After strokes of fate or after major changes, such as those caused by the Corona crisis, the question of the meaning of life arises again for many people. From my point of view, there is no one and only sense, the ultimate purpose of life. If this existed, life would become absolutely meaningless once this goal has been achieved. For me it turns out that during all the years of your life there is not only one meaning, but that the respective main meaning can also change. If, in short, the meaning of a toddler's life is based on learning to walk and talk, then it is to be learned and socialized during school time. After that, the meaning of life is mainly to get a job, find a life partner, rent or buy an apartment or build a house and possibly raise children. Whenever one of these goals is achieved, there must be a reorientation; otherwise there is a risk of getting stuck somehow in personal development. Moving out of the children, or now more often the only child, becomes a big question of meaning for many mothers. Especially when they are not at work and only at home, this was much more common in the past. Suddenly, sometimes even from one day to the next, the meaning of life for the past twenty years or more is no longer there, they fall into a deep hole and under certain circumstances become really depressed. The situation is similar for many (mainly men) with the pension shock.

Not only in this situation it is important that everyone gives themselves a (main) sense and several secondary senses. In many cases, these new senses or goals do not have to be useful and profitable from an economic point of view. If the economic and financial basis is in place, then it is certainly time to return to your often hidden or forgotten talents and interests. I know one case where the art education teacher kept

63

explaining to this girl that she couldn't paint, that she was an artistic anti-talent just because she didn't paint the way the teacher had imagined. The years and decades passed without her ever picking up a brush again. Why should she have done it too? However, she used many other artistic techniques and produced really great results. When her children had been away from home for a long time and her employment was over, her husband asked for a picture of her for his 70th birthday, because he was convinced that with her artistic streak she too should be able to paint. The result of her first attempt at painting was simply stunning. Since then she has painted many pictures with acrylic and oil. Painting is not the meaning of her life now, but it has brought additional meaning, joy and variety to her life.

More than two thousand years ago, the Roman poet Horace summed up his wisdom in two words: "carpe diem" – usually translated as "use the day". Even if the benefit corresponds more to the Christian-Western way of life, there is still a not insignificant difference to the original meaning "pick the day". It is a metaphor and is intended to express the picking and collecting of ripe fruits or flowers, i.e. to enjoy the moment without exertion, as it is e.g. present in the sensual experience of nature. Actually, this is a paradisiacal state, where you don't have to work the ground in the sweat of your face, but are happy and satisfied with what nature offers you. People who get off the treadmill are often disparagingly referred to as life artists. It is a real compliment if someone understands the art of living and is not a failure or a "life bungler". Unfortunately, in school we are only stuffed with a lot of – sometimes very questionable – knowledge, but the art of living, being happy and content, is not taught.

As early as the 18th century there was a statement in the legal code of Bhutan, a small kingdom in the Himalayas, which should actually apply to all countries on earth: "If the government cannot create happiness for its people, then there is no reason for the existence of this government. "The factors for national happiness in Bhutan are: social justice, cultural freedom, legal equality and ecological sustainability, but not wealth and prosperity. The first three are very reminiscent of the battle cry of the French Revolution with freedom, equality and fraternity. Unfortunately, these values have often been twisted in the West and freedom of action only applies to global corporations and their tax freedom. The equality applies above all to the broad masses in terms of their largely equally low income and low wealth. For the most part, fraternity is only practiced in the various lobby groups, lodges and political parties for their own benefit and at the expense of the people. We cannot expect them to give up their privileges of their own free will. But each of us can contribute in our own area to make the world a more peaceful place, to make us all a little happier and more content.

YOU are the center of your universe; it depends on YOU, and be the starting point for change for the better:

Carpe diem – enjoy the day!

Publications of the
Vienna Historical Society
(Geschichtswissenschaftlichen Gesellschaft Wien)

All books are originally published in German.
Editions in English are in preparation for some oft the titles.

All books are available directly from the publisher's shop:
www.bod.de/buchshop/, in any bookstore or on the Internet

Hans Gruber, Leo Munt, John Seberg, Rüdiger Seten und Yvonne Wayne

Der Maya-Kalender 3114 v.Chr.-2100 n.Chr.

Haab - Tzolkin - Long Count für jeden einzelnen Tag

The Mayan Calendar 3114 BC - 2100 AD

Haab - Tzolkin - Long Count for every single day

The accompanying text is only in German!

Interest in the Mayan calendar has increased over the past few years and decades. And not only in specialist groups, but above all in a broad audience. So far there have only been relatively expensive editions of individual years of the Maya calendar, but no really comprehensive representation of the three Mayan calendar systems valid next to one another for each individual day, namely the Tzolkin and Haab calendars and the Long Count.

With this series of books we want to fill this gap and provide an inexpensive complete edition of the Mayan calendar from its beginning in 3114 BC. Until the end of this century.

Each volume comprises 100 years on three double pages, the volume with the beginning of the calendar comprises 114 years. Until the Gregorian calendar reform on 4th / 15th October 1582 is the basis of the Julian calendar, then the Gregorian. In addition to the "calendar of the century", there are also special editions for the years 2001-2020, 2021-2030 and 2021-2050.

There were five of us working on this work, with one team member ultimately responsible for each band, so we decided to only mention this one as the author of the respective band.

The team consists of Hans Gruber, Leo Munt, John Seberg, Rüdiger Seten and Yvonne Wayne, each of whom brought their special knowledge and skills to the project so that it could succeed. We hope that this work is helpful in your chronological studies!

Sonderausgaben - special editions:

John Seberg

Der Maya-Kalender 2021-2030 n.Chr.

John Seberg

Der Maya-Kalender 2021-2050 n.Chr.

These books are only published in German!

Erhard Zauner

DIE UNHEILIGE SCHRIFT

Die Kriminalgeschichte von Jahwe und seinem auserwählten Volk – oder –
Was wirklich in der Bibel steht: Von der Schöpfung bis zum Auszug aus Ägypten

Wer glaubt, dass die Bibel eine „Heilige Schrift" sei, die das barmherzige Wirken des lieben, guten Gottes schildert, der von Anbeginn an durch alle Zeiten für alle Menschen da ist, der hat sie nicht gelesen. Das Gegenteil ist wahr. In dieser „UN-heiligen Schrift" finden wir alle verabscheuungswürdigen Verbrechen wie Krieg, Mord, Menschenopfer, Lüge, Betrug, Ehebruch, Polygamie, Inzucht, Frauenfeindlichkeit, Genitalverstümmelung, Menschenhandel, Sklaverei, Rassismus, Fremdenhass, Götzenanbetung, Rache, Raub und vielfachen Völkermord. Begangen werden all diese Verbrechen von Jahwe selbst, von seinem auserwählten Volk oder den Säulenheiligen des Alten Testaments, zumeist sogar noch von Jahwe selbst dazu angestiftet. Obwohl diese

zigmal Jahwes Gebote und Gesetze brechen, werden sie dafür nicht bestraft, während einfache Menschen oft wegen kleinster Vergehen von Jahwe selbst getötet werden. Jahwes Auftreten, sein Verhalten und sein Charakter sind so unterschiedlich, dass man davon ausgehen muss, dass der Jahwe der Schöpfung und des Paradieses, der Jahwe der Sintflut, der Jahwe der Patriarchenzeit und der Jahwe der Ägyptischen Plagen und des Auszuges nie und nimmer ein und dieselbe Person (oder Gott) gewesen sein können. Wussten Sie,

• dass es zwei gänzlich unterschiedliche Versionen der Schöpfung gibt?
• dass die verfluchte Schlange später von den Israeliten verehrt und ihr geopfert wurde?
• dass Jahwe in der Bibel achtzehn mal einen Bund schließt und keinen einzigen hält?
• dass Abraham seine Schwester heiratet und sie mit zwei weiteren Männern vermählt?
• dass Jakob mit zwei Schwestern und zwei weiteren Frauen gleichzeitig verheiratet ist?
• dass Mose einen Mord begangen hat, bevor er zum Religionsgründer wird?
• dass Jahwe Mose zum Gott für den Pharao macht?
• dass Jahwe Hörner wie ein Wildstier hat?
• dass Jahwe sich selbst nicht als Gott aller Menschen, sondern nur der Israeliten betrachtet?
• dass Jahwe sich jahrhundertlang nicht einmal um sein auserwähltes Volk gekümmert hat?
• dass Jahwe millionenfache Genitalverstümmelung verlangt, und Jesus dies gutheißt?

The English edition of this book is in preparation!

Erhard Zauner

THE UN HOLY SCRIPTURE

The criminal story of Yahweh and his chosen people - or -
What is really in the Bible: From creation to the exodus from Egypt

Anyone who believes that the Bible is a "holy scripture" that describes the merciful work of the dear, good God, who has been there for all people from the beginning through all times, has not read it. The opposite is true. In this "UN Holy Scripture" we find all despicable crimes such as war, murder, human sacrifice, lies, fraud, adultery, polygamy, inbreeding, misogyny, genital mutilation, human trafficking, slavery, racism, xenophobia, idol worship, revenge, robbery and multiple genocide. All these crimes are committed by Yahweh himself, by his chosen people or the pillar saints of the Old Testament, mostly even instigated by Yahweh himself. Although these dozens of times break Yahweh's commandments and laws, they are not punished for it, while ordinary people are often killed by Yahweh himself for the smallest offenses. Yahweh's appearance, behavior and character are so different that one has to assume that the Yahweh of creation and Paradise, the Yahweh of the Flood, the Yahweh of the Patriarchal Period and the Yahweh of the Plagues of Egypt and the Exodus never ever could have been the same person (or God). Did you know…

• that there are two completely different versions of creation?

• that the cursed serpent was later worshiped and sacrificed by the Israelites?

• that Yahweh makes a covenant 18 times and does not keep a single one?

• that Abraham marries his sister and wed her to two other men?

• that Jacob is married to two sisters and two other women at the same time?

• that Moses committed murder before he became a founder of the religion?

• that Yahweh made Moses God for Pharaoh?

• that Yahweh has horns like a wild bull?

• that Yahweh does not regard himself as God of all people, but only of the Israelites?

• that Yahweh did not even care for his chosen people for centuries?

• that Yahweh demands millions of genital mutilation and that Jesus approves of it?

69

Erhard Zauner

EXODUS

Der mehrfache Auszug der Juden aus Ägypten nach
biblischen, außerbiblischen und ägyptischen Quellen

Erhard Zauner

EXODUS

Der mehrfache Auszug
der Juden aus Ägypten nach
biblischen, außerbiblischen
und ägyptischen Quellen

Aufgrund eines völlig neuen Ansatzes gelingt es dem Autor die biblische Geschichte von Abraham bis David in ein komplett neues Licht zu rücken. Der lückenlose Stammbaum aller Nachkommen von Jakob bis König David zeigt, dass sich das gesamte Geschehen, das in der Bibel, je nach Zählung, zwischen 400 und 1000 Jahre dauert, effektiv innerhalb von nur 10 Generationen oder etwa 200 Jahren abspielt. Erst mit der um 300 Jahre verkürzten ägyptischen Chronologie wird die biblische Geschichte nachvollziehbar. Unter Berücksichtigung von außerbiblischen Berichten vom Exodus können Parallelen in der ägyptischen Geschichte und Literatur gefunden werden.

Die biblische Geschichte ist ein Patchwork von verschiedenen Erzählungen, die am Gerüst des fiktiven Stammbaumes von Abraham befestigt wurden. Trennt man diese, so können viele Stellen des AT der ägyptischen Geschichte zuordnet werden, allerdings in einer komplett anderen Reihenfolge. Das führt zur Erkenntnis, dass es mehrere Auszüge verschiedener Gruppen zu verschiedenen Zeiten unter unterschiedlichen Bedingungen gibt. Der erste Exodus findet am Ende der 6. Dynastie, der nächste am Ende der 12. Dynastie anlässlich der Katastrophe durch den Ausbruch des Vulkans Thera statt. Diese Katastrophe findet sich in den ägyptischen Plagen wieder.

Weitere Auszüge gibt es während der 18. Dynastie bei der Vertreibung der Hyksos, unter Amenophis III. (Zeit von König David) und bei Tutanchamun. Unter dem goldenen Pharao kommt es zu einer antiken Verschwörung und nach der Auffindung seines Grabes zu einer zweiten, neuzeitlichen Verschwörung.

70

The English edition of this book is in preparation!

Erhard Zauner

EXODUS

The multiple exodus of the Jews from Egypt according to biblical, extra-biblical, and Egyptian sources

Thanks to a completely new approach, the author succeeds in shedding a completely new light on the biblical story from Abraham to David. The complete family tree of all descendants from Jacob to King David shows that the entire event, which, depending on the count, lasts between 400 and 1000 years in the Bible, effectively takes place within only 10 generations or around 200 years. Only with the Egyptian chronology shortened by 300 years does the biblical story become comprehensible. Taking into account extra-biblical descriptions of the Exodus, parallels can be found in Egyptian history and literature.

The biblical history is a patchwork of different narratives attached to the framework of the fictional family tree of Abraham. If these branches are separated, many parts of the Old Testament can be assigned to Egyptian history, but in a completely different order. This leads to the realization that there are several exoduses from different groups at different times under different conditions. The first exodus takes place at the end of the 6th dynasty, the next at the end of the 12th dynasty on the occasion of the catastrophe caused by the eruption of the Thera volcano. This catastrophe can be found in the plagues of Egypt.

There are further exoduses during the 18th dynasty with the expulsion of the Hyksos, under Amenhotep III. (time of King David) and with Tutankhamun. An ancient conspiracy ensues under the golden pharaoh and, after his grave has been found, a second, modern conspiracy.

71

Erhard Zauner

Autonomes und lebenslanges Lernen: ein modernes, 2000 Jahre altes, Prinzip

Jüdische Erziehung und Unterricht in der Zeit um Christi Geburt unter besonderer Berücksichtigung der essenischen Schriftfunde vom Toten Meer

Dieses Buch ist eine fächerübergreifende Arbeit, die vom Urchristentum, besser gesagt vom Übergang vom Judentum zum Christentum und von der wissenschaftlichen Pädagogik handelt. Was auf den ersten Blick vielleicht als nur von historischem Interesse scheint, stellt sich bei genauerer Betrachtung in zweifacher Weise als aktuell heraus:

1. Aufgrund der Rollenfunde vom Toten Meer haben wir Einblicke in das jüdische Leben in der Zeit um Christi Geburt erhalten, die 2000 Jahre unverändert erhalten geblieben sind und daher keinerlei Zensur oder „Verschlimmbesserung" unterworfen waren.

2. Die beiden pädagogischen Grundprinzipien der Juden schlechthin, nämlich die Anleitung zum selbständigen Lernen und das lebenslange Lernen werden heute in der pädagogischen Literatur oft gefordert, aber noch viel zu selten und wenig effizient umgesetzt, haben jedoch im Judentum einen mindestens zweitausendjährigen erfolgreichen Praxistest hinter sich.

Hier könnte viel in kurzer Zeit bewegt werden, würde man die bewährte Methode übernehmen. Dabei gäbe es allerdings ein Problem: Diese beiden Grundwerte werden den jüdischen Kindern von ihren Müttern bereits mit der Muttermilch verabreicht. Man müsste also zuerst die Eltern erziehen, wie es J. W. Goethe sagt: „Man könnt' erzogene Kinder gebären, wenn die Eltern erzogen wären." (Zahme Xenien IV. 1113-1114)

72

The English edition of this book is in preparation!

Erhard Zauner

Autonomous and Lifelong Learning: a Modern, 2000 Year old, Principle

Jewish education and instruction in the time around the birth of Christ with special consideration of the Essenian writings from the Dead Sea

This book is an interdisciplinary work that deals with early Christianity, or rather the transition from Judaism to Christianity, and with scientific pedagogy. What at first glance might appear to be of historical interest only turns out to be current in two ways on closer inspection:

1. Due to the scroll finds from the Dead Sea, we have gained insights into Jewish life around the time of the birth of Christ, which have remained unchanged for 2000 years and were therefore not subject to any censorship or "awful improvement"

2. The two basic educational principles of the Jews par excellence, namely instructions for independent learning and lifelong learning, are often required in educational literature today, but are still implemented far too rarely and inefficiently, but have successfully passed practical tests for at least two thousand years in Judaism .

A lot could be moved here in a short time if the tried and tested method were adopted. There would be a problem with this, however: These two basic values are given to Jewish children by their mothers in their mother's milk. So you would have to raise your parents first, as the German poet Goethe says: "You could give birth to educated children if the parents were educated." (Zahme Xenien IV. 1113-1114)

Erhard Zauner

Die Templer, Baphomet, das Turiner Grabtuch und der Heilige Gral

Eine neue Sicht auf 2000 Jahre Geschichte

The German edition of this book will be published soon!

The English edition of this book is in preparation!

Erhard Zauner

The Templars, Baphomet, the Turin Shroud and the Holy Grail

A new view at 2000 years of history

Erhard Zauner

Die Jesus Sensation

Die Entschlüsselung des essenischen Sonnenkalenders
von Qumran und der Chronologie der Evangelien

Die Lösung des größten Rätsels der Menschheit

Erhard Zauner

Die
Jesus
Sensation

Die Entschlüsselung des essenischen
Sonnenkalenders von Qumran
und der Chronologie der Evangelien

Die Lösung des größten
Rätsels der Menschheit

Nach fünfzigjähriger Beschäftigung ist es dem Autor erstmals gelungen, mit Hilfe von Angaben aus den Schriftrollen vom Toten Meer, des Talmuds und des Neuen Testaments, eine eindeutige Zuordnung des essenischen Sonnenkalenders von Qumran zum julianischen Kalender zu erstellen und zu beweisen.

Johannes der Täufer und Jesus haben demnach die Feste nach diesem Qumran-Kalender gefeiert. Ebenso wurden ihre Zeugungs-, Geburts-, Kreuzigungs- bzw. Sterbedaten danach tradiert. Mit nur ganz wenigen Adaptierungen lassen sich praktisch alle chronologischen Angaben der Evangelien und der außerbiblischen Schriften in diesem Sonnenkalender in eine sinnvolle stimmige Abfolge bringen. Das Ergebnis wird allerdings für manche sehr überraschend sein, da sich vieles damals eben nicht so abgespielt hat, wie es in liebevoller Tradition verbreitet wird. Außerdem wurde der offizielle Tempelkult zumindest bis kurz vor die Zeitenwende auch nach dem Qumrankalender zelebriert.

Johannes und Jesus stehen voll und ganz in der jüdischen Tradition und haben nie und nimmer jene neue Religion begründet, die als Christentum weltweite Verbreitung gefunden hat. Diese Verfälschung der urchristlichen Lehre von Johannes und Jesus geht primär auf Paulus, dann auf die Diener des römischen Kaiserhofes und in der Folge auf die Katholische Kirche, den Vatikan und die machtbesessenen Päpste zurück.

The German edition of this book will be published soon!

76

The English edition of this book is in preparation!

Erhard Zauner

The Jesus Sensation

The deciphering of the Essenian solar calendar
of Qumran and the chronology of the Gospels

The solution to humankind's greatest mystery

After fifty years, the author has succeeded for the first time, with informations from the Dead Sea Scrolls, the Talmud and the New Testament, to create and prove a clear correlation between the Essenian solar calendar of Qumran and the Julian calendar.

So he can definitely state that John the Baptist and Jesus celebrated the feasts according to this Qumran calendar. Their dates of begatting, birth, crucifixion and death were also passed on afterwards. With just a few adaptations, practically all chronological information from the Gospels and the extra-biblical writings can be put into a meaningful, coherent sequence in this solar calendar. The result will, however, be very surprising for some, as a lot of things did not happen back then as it is spread in loving tradition. In addition, the official temple cult was celebrated according to the Qumran calendar, at least until shortly before the new era.

John and Jesus stand completely in the Jewish tradition and have never, ever founded that new religion which, as Christianity, has spread throughout the world. This falsification of the early Christian doctrine of John and Jesus is primarily due to Paul, then to the servants of the Roman imperial court and subsequently to the Catholic Church, the Vatican and the power-obsessed popes.

Studien zur Philosophie von Karl Popper 1
Erhard Zauner
Die offene Bildungsgesellschaft und ihre Feinde
Poppers Gesellschaftskritik mit Blick auf das Bildungssystem

Studies on the philosophy of Karl Popper 1
The open educational society and its enemies
Popper's criticism of society with a view to the education system

Studien zur Philosophie von Karl Popper 2
Erhard Zauner
Eine kritische Betrachtung der Theorien von Karl Raimund Popper
Die Weiterentwicklung des »kritischen« zum »toleranten« Rationalismus
und der »offenen« zur »offenen toleranten« Gesellschaft

Studies on the philosophy of Karl Popper 2
A critical look at the theories of Karl Raimund Popper
The further development of the "critical" to the "tolerant" rationalism
and the "open" to the "open tolerant" society

Studien zur Philosophie von Karl Popper 3
Erhard Zauner
Die offene tolerante Gesellschaft mit human-kapitalistischer Marktwirtschaft
Entwurf einer neuen gerechteren Wirtschafts- und
Gesellschaftsordnung basierend auf Volks-Souveränität,
individueller Freiheit und minimaler staatlicher Intervention

Studies on the philosophy of Karl Popper 3
The open, tolerant society with a human capitalist market economy
Draft of a new, more just economic and social order based on people's sovereignty, individual freedom and minimal government intervention

These three book will only be published in German!

78